I0021785

Deep Learning for Beginners with TensorFlow

The basics

Mark Smart

Copyright©2018 Mark Smart
All Rights Reserved

Copyright © 2018 by Mark Smart

All rights reserved. No part of this publication may be reproduced, distributed, or transmitted in any form or by any means, including photocopying, recording, or other electronic or mechanical methods, without the prior written permission of the author, except in the case of brief quotations embodied in critical reviews and certain other noncommercial uses permitted by copyright law.

Tags: deep learning with python, tensorflow machine learning, tensorflow deep learning cookbook, tensorflow for deep learning, programming book, tensorflow for dummies, tensorflow books, machine learning with tensorflow, tensorflow c++, concept of graphs, neural network, neural networks python, tensorflow with neural network, tensorflow python.

Table of Contents

Disclaimer

While all attempts have been made to verify the information provided in this book, the author does assume any responsibility for errors, omissions, or contrary interpretations of the subject matter contained within. The information provided in this book is for educational and entertainment purposes only. The reader is responsible for his or her own actions and the author does not accept any responsibilities for any liabilities or damages, real or perceived, resulting from the use of this information.

The trademarks that are used are without any consent, and the publication of the trademark is without permission or backing by the trademark owner. All trademarks and brands within this book are for clarifying purposes only and are the owned by the owners themselves, not affiliated with this document.

Introduction

Deep learning is one of the fields of machine learning. Machine learning refers to the ability of computers to learn from experience. Research has shown that computers can learn when exposed to data. The result of this is an improvement in performance. In deep learning, we create neural network computer models to learn from data. These normally work from the inspiration of how the human brain works. TensorFlow is a deep learning library that can be used in Python, C++ and other programming languages. This book helps you understand deep learning in Python using TensorFlow. Enjoy reading!

Chapter 1- Getting started

What is TensorFlow?

TensorFlow refers to a framework from Goggle used for creation of deep learning models. TensorFlow relies on data-flow graphs for numerical computation. TensorFlow has made machine learning easy. It makes the processes of acquiring data, training machine learning models, making predictions and modifying future results easy.

The library was developed by the Google's Brain team for use in large-scale machine learning. TensorFlow brings together machine learning and deep learning algorithms and models and it makes them much useful via a common metaphor. TensorFlow uses Python to give its users a front-end API that can be used for building applications, with the applications being executed in high-performance C++.

TensorFlow can be used for building, training and running deep neural networks for image recognition, handwritten digit classification, recurrent neural networks, word embedding, natural language processing etc.

How it Works

Tensors helps its users create dataflow graphs, which are structures describing the flow of data between graphs or processing nodes arranged in a series. Every node in the graph is a representation of a mathematical operation, and every edge connecting nodes is a representation of a tensor or multidimensional data array.

All of these are provided to the users via Python programming language. It is easy for one to learn Python, and provides an easy way of understanding how high-level abstractions can be put together. In TensorFlow, all tensors and nodes are Python objects, while the TensorFlow applications are Python applications.

However, the math operations are not done in Python. The TensorFlow libraries used for transformations are written in high-performance C++ binaries.

The work of Python is to direct traffic between them, and provides abstractions to connect them. Applications developed in TensorFlow can be used on any convenient platform such as a cloud cluster, local machine, and CPUS, GPUs, Android and iOS devices. The models created in models can be used on a wide variety of devices for making predictions.

Why should you use TensorFlow?

One of the greatest advantages of using TensorFlow is the abstraction it offers. Instead of being concerned with the low-level details regarding the implementation of algorithms, or looking for a proper way of channeling the output from a function as input to another function, the developer is allowed to focus on the entire logic concerning the application under development. TensorFlow then takes care of the rest of the details.

TensorFlow also provides developers with an additional convenience when debugging their apps. It has the eager execution mode that allows one to evaluate every graph operation transparently and separately rather than having to make the whole graph as a single object then analyzing it at a go.

What is Deep Learning?

Deep learning is a branch of machine learning that relies on algorithms that works to mimic the way the human brain operates, resulting into artificial neural networks.
Deep learning has inspired implementations like driverless cars, making them differentiate between pedestrians and posts and even recognize stop signs. It is also the technology behind voice recognition applications used in tablets, phones, TVs and speakers. With deep learning, computer models are able to perform classification tasks from text, images or sound.

The deep learning models can provide a high level of accuracy, sometimes outperforming humans. Training of models is done using large sets of labeled data and neural networks with several layers.

Most methods for deep learning use neural networks, hence deep learning models are usually referred to as *deep neural networks.*

The word "deep" refers to the number of hidden layers that a neural network has. Most neural networks have 2-3 hidden layers, but a deep neural network may have over 100 hidden layers. Training of such models involves the use of large sets of data. Neural network architectures with no need for manual intervention are then used to extract patterns from the data.

A good example of a deep neural network is the convolution neural network (CNN).
A CNN uses 2D convolution layers, which makes it good for processing of 2D data like images. With CNN, there is no need for extracting features manually as you are not required to identify the features to be used for classifying images. CNNs directly extract features from images. The ability of deep learning models to extract features automatically makes them suitable for use in computer vision problems like object classification.

The CNNs rely on numerous layers to detect the features of an image. The complexity of the image features increases at every layer.

In the first hidden layer for example, the edges of the mages may be detected while the last layer may learn complex features in the image.

A good example of application of deep learning is in fraud detection systems. Once it learns the normal procedures, any anomaly will be easily detected and classified as a potential for fraud.

Installing TensorFlow

You now know the details of TensorFlow; hence you can install the library. TensorFlow comes with APIs for programming languages like C++, Haskell, Go, Java, Rust, and it comes with a third-party package for R known as *tensorflow*.

We will be guiding you on how to install TensorFlow on Windows. On Windows, TensorFlow can be installed with pip or Anaconda.

The native pip will install the TensorFlow on your system without having to go through a virtual environment. However, note that installation of TensorFlow with pip may interfere with other Python installations on your system. However, the good thing is that you only have to run a single command and TensorFlow will be installed on your system. Also, when TensorFlow is installed via pip, users will be allowed to run the TensorFlow programs from the directory they want.

To install TensorFlow with Anaconda, you may have to create a virtual environment. However, within the Anaconda itself, it is recommended that you install TensorFlow via the *pip install* command rather than the *conda install* command.

Ensure that you have installed Python 3.5 and above on your Windows system. Python3 comes with pip3 program which can be used for installation of TensorFlow. This means we should use the *pip3 install* command for installation purposes. The following command will help you install CPU-only version for TensorFlow:

pip3 install --upgrade tensorflow

The command should be run from the command line:

```
C:\Windows\system32>pip3 install --upgrade tensorflow
Collecting tensorflow
  Downloading https://files.pythonhosted.org/packages/3f/bb/dd01844cf88d15264d92
e12a8b89526e1d805c082b8e945b632d4a1989a4/tensorflow-1.8.0-cp35-cp35m-win_amd64.w
hl (34.4MB)
    16% |#####                           | 5.7MB 290kB/s eta 0:01:39
```

If you need to install a GPU version for TensorFlow, run this command:

pip3 install --upgrade tensorflow-gpu

This will install TensorFlow on your Windows system.

Validating TensorFlow Installation

You should verify whether the installation of TensorFlow was successful or not. Open the Python command prompt then run the following sequence of commands:

>>> import tensorflow as tf
>>> hello = tf.constant('Hello, this is TensorFlow!')
>>> ses = tf.Session()
>>> print(ses.run(hello))

The code should print the following:

Hello, this is TensorFlow!

If the code prints the above, then you have successfully installed TensorFlow on your Windows system. Congratulation!

Chapter 2- Building a Neural Network

TensorFlow is good for tasks about deep learning. It may also be run on multiple CPUs or GPUs, and this makes it suitable for complex deep learning problems. In this chapter, we will be discussing the basics of building neural networks in Python with TensorFlow. We will create a neural network with three layers to work on our dataset.

TensorFlow Graphs

In TensorFlow, computation is based on graphs. The graphs provide us with an alternative for soling mathematical problems. Consider the expression given below:

x = (y+z) * (z+4)

The above expression may also be expressed as follows:

p=y + z
q= z + 4
x= p * q

When represented as above, it becomes easy to express the expression in the form of a graph. This shown below:

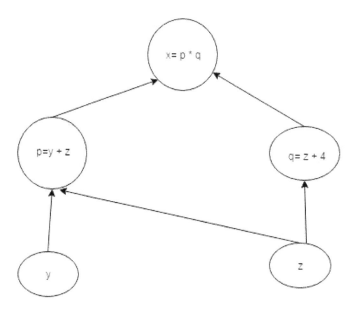

Initially, we had a single expression but we now have two expressions. The two expressions can be performed in parallel. We can gain from this in terms of computation time. Such gains are very important in deep learning and big data applications, especially in Convolutional Neural Networks (CNNs) and Recurrent Neural Networks (RNNs) which are all complicated neural network architectures.

The goal of TensorFlow is to implement graphs and help in the computation of operations in parallel which will lead into efficiency gains. In TensorFlow, the graph nodes are known as *tensors* and they are simply multi-dimensional data arrays. The graph begins with the input layer where we find the input tensor. After the input layer, we get the hidden layer which has rectified linear units as activation function.

We need to use our previous equation, that is, $x = (y+z) * (z+4)$, to demonstrate how TensorFlow handles it. You first be familiar with variables and constants in TensorFlow. Let us begin by declaring them:

import tensorflow as tf
 # Begin by creating a TensorFlow constant
const = tf.constant(2.0, name="const")
 # create the TensorFlow variables
y = tf.Variable(2.0, name='y')
z = tf.Variable(1.0, name='z')

To declare constants in TensorFlow, we use the tf.constant function, while variables are declared using the tf.Variable function. We begin with the value to be assigned to the constant or variable once it has been initialized. We then have the optional name string for labeling the variable or constant. The type for the variable or constant will be inferred from the value you assign to it. However, you can use the dtype argument to set it explicitly, but this is optional. There are various types in TensorFlow including tf.float32, tf.int32 etc.

With standard Python, the above variables and constants will have not been declared. Due to this, variables, constants, operations and computational graph are only created once the initialization commands are executed.

Next, we can create the TensorFlow operations:

 # Let us create the operations
p = tf.add(y, z, name='p')

```
q = tf.add(z, const, name='q')
x = tf.multiply(p, q, name='x')
```

TensorFlow provides you with numerous operations that can help you perform various operations on your variables.

Next, we can setup an object that will be used for initializing the variables as well as the graph structure. Here it is:

```
# creating a variable initialization
init_op = tf.global_variables_initializer()
```

We are now ready for the next step. To execute operations between our variables, we are required to launch a TensorFlow session, that is, *tf.session*. The TensorFlow session provides an object in which we will run our operations.
We can use the Python syntax for *with* and run the graph as follows:

```
# Launch the session
with tf.Session() as ses:
    # initialize the variables
    ses.run(init_op)
    # calculate the graph output
    x_out = ses.run(x)
    print("Variable x is {}".format(x_out))
```

We have the *run* command within the code given above. The next steps involve figuring what our variable x should be. We only need to run the operation that calculates x, which is $x = tf.multiply(p, q, name='x')$. In this case, x is an operation rather than a variable, hence we can run it. To do this, we have used the ses.run(x) command and the output has been assigned to x_out, and we print the value of this.

Note that we have defined the operations p and q which must be calculated before figuring out what x is. However, there is no need for us to run those operations explicitly since TensorFlow is aware of the variables and operations that x depends on, hence it will run the required operations on its own. This is done through data flow graph which will show it all the needed dependencies.
We can use the TensorBoard functionality to get the graph that TensorFlow created for us.

TensorFlow Placeholder

Suppose we are not aware of the value of array y during declaration phase of our TensorFlow problem, that is, before the stage for tf.Session() as ses. In such a case, TensorFlow expects us to declare basic structure of our data by use of tf.placeholder variable declaration. We can use it for y as shown below:

 # creating TensorFlow variables
y = tf.placeholder(tf.float32, [None, 1], name='y')

Since we are not providing any initialization in the declaration, we should notify TensorFlow the data type of every element within the tensor. Our aim is to use tf.float32. Our second argument denotes the shape of the data to be injected in the variable. We need to use an array of size (? x 1). Since we don't know the amount of data to supply to the array, we have used the "?". The placeholder is ready to accept None argument for the size declaration. After that, we are now able to inject any amount of 1-dimensional data we need into variable y.

Our program also expects a change in ses.run(x,...). This is shown below:

x_out = ses.run(x, feed_dict={y: np.arange(0, 10)[:, np.newaxis]})

Note that the argument feed_dict has been added to the command ses.run(x,...). We have removed the mystery and we have specified what the variable y is expected to be, which is 1-dimensional range between 0 and 10. As the argument name suggests, feed_dict, the input we are to supply is a Python dictionary, and every key will be the placeholder name that we are going to fill.

Now you are done and you have implemented a graph in TensorFlow. You should have the following code:

import tensorflow as tf
import numpy as np

```
# Begin by creating a TensorFlow constant
const = tf.constant(2.0, name="const")
# create the TensorFlow variables
y = tf.Variable(2.0, name='y')
z = tf.Variable(1.0, name='z')
# Let us create the operations
p = tf.add(y, z, name='p')
q = tf.add(z, const, name='q')
x = tf.multiply(p, q, name='x')
# creating a variable initialization
init_op = tf.global_variables_initializer()
# Launch the session
with tf.Session() as ses:
    # initialize the variables
    ses.run(init_op)
    # calculate the graph output
    x_out = ses.run(x)
    print("Variable x is {}".format(x_out))
# creating TensorFlow variables

y = tf.placeholder(tf.float32, [None, 1], name='y')

x_out = ses.run(x, feed_dict={y: np.arange(0, 10)[:, np.newaxis]})
```

Building neural Networks

We will be demonstrating how you can a neural network with 3 layers in TensorFlow. We will use the MNIST dataset which serves as the "hello world" dataset for deep learning projects.

This dataset is provided by the TensorFlow package. It has 28 /8 28 grayscale image all with handwritten digits. The dataset has 55,000 training rows, 5,000 validation rows and 10,000 testing rows.

The following lines of code can help us to load the dataset:

from tensorflow.examples.tutorials.mnist import input_data

mnistData = input_data.read_data_sets("MNIST_data/", one_hot=True)

The argument one_hot=True states that rather than the labels associated with every image being digit itself, that is, 4, it's a vector with a "one hot" node with the rest of the nodes being 0, that is, [0, 0, 0, 0, 1, 0, 0, 0, 0, 0]. This makes it easy for one to load it into output layer of their neural network.

We can create placeholder variables for our training data:

```
# Optimization variables
learning_rate = 0.5
epochs = 10
batch_size = 100
# Create placeholders for training data
# input a - for 28 x 28 pixels = 784
a = tf.placeholder(tf.float32, [None, 784])
```

 # now create the placeholder for output data - 10 digits
b = tf.placeholder(tf.float32, [None, 10])

Note that the x input layer is 784 nodes corresponding to the 28 * 28 pixels, which equals to 784. The "?" has been used to represented the unknown number of inputs that are to be used. The b output layer has 10 units which correspond 10 possible digits. Again, has a size of (? * 784), which represents an unknown number of inputs, marking the function of *placeholder* variable.

It is now time for us to set the bias and weight variables for our neural network. The number of weights/bias tensors always equals L-1, where L is the total number of layers. In our case, we will be setting up two tensors for each of them:

 # we can declare the weights connecting our input to hidden layer

W1 = tf.Variable(tf.random_normal([784, 300], stddev=0.03), name='W1')

y1 = tf.Variable(tf.random_normal([300]), name='y1')

 # then the weights connecting hidden layer to output layer

W2 = tf.Variable(tf.random_normal([300, 10], stddev=0.03), name='W2')

y2 = tf.Variable(tf.random_normal([10]), name='y2')

We began by declaring some variables, W1 and y1, representing the weights and the bias between the input and the hidden layer respectively. Our network should have 300 nodes in its hidden layer, so W1, which is the size for weight sensor will be [784, 300]. The values for the weights have been initialized using random normal distribution having a mean of 0 and a standard deviation of 0.03. We have also created the W2 and y2 variables to help in connecting the hidden layer of the network to the output layer.

Next, we should setup the node inputs and the activation functions for the nodes of the hidden layer. This is shown below:

```
# get the output of hidden layer
hidden_out = tf.add(tf.matmul(a, W1), y1)
hidden_out = tf.nn.relu(hidden_out)
```

In first line above, we have executed a matrix multiplication of weights (W1) by input vector a then we added the bias $y1$. We used the tf.matmul operation to run the multiplication of the matrix. The hidden_out operation has then been finalized by application of rectified linear unit activation to matrix multiplication then the bias. TensorFlow comes with a rectified linear unit activation that has readily been setup for us, which is named tf.nn.relu.

We can now proceed to setup the output layer, which is y_:

 # now compute the output for hidden layer – we will use a softmax #activated output layer

b_ = tf.nn.softmax(tf.add(tf.matmul(hidden_out, W2), y2))

We have again done the weight multiplication with the output obtained from hidden layer (hidden_out) followed by addition of the bias, y2. The softmax activation has been used for the output layer, which comes included in TensorFlow and named TF.NN.SOFTMAX.

A cost or loss function must also be included for backpropagation/optimization to work on. The cross entropy function should be used for this case. The following TensorFlow code can help us implement the cross entropy function:

b_clipped = tf.clip_by_value(b_, 1e-10, 0.9999999)

cross_entropy = - tf.reduce_mean(tf.reduce_sum(b * tf.log(b_clipped)+ (1 - b) * tf.log(1 - b_clipped), axis=1))

The first line is an operation that helps us convert the output b_ to clipped version, which will be limited between 1e-10 and 0.999999.

This helps us avoid having log(0) during the operation when performing the training, which returns NaN and breaks the process of training. The second line above is simply a cross entropy calculation.

To perform the calculation, we use the tf.reduce_sum function provided by TensorFlow. The function takes the sum of the given axis for the tensor that you supply. In our case, the supplied tensor is element-wise cross-entropy calculation for single node and training sample. The b and b_clipped are (m * 10) tensors. Hence we should get the first sum over second axis. To specify this, we use the axis==1 argument, in which 1 denotes the second axis in cases where there is a system with zero-based indices in Python.

After that operation, we will have the (m x 1) tensor. To get the tensors mean and complete the cross entropy cost calculation, we should call the tf.reduce_mean function of TensorFlow. The function will take the mean of any tensor that you provide. We now have a cost function that may be used for training purpose.

First, let us set the optimizer:

Add the optimizer
**optimizer =
tf.train.GradientDescentOptimizer(learning_rate
=learning_rate).minimize(cross_entropy)**

We have used the gradient descent optimizer provided to us by TensorFlow. It should be initialized with the learning rate, hen define what it should do, which is simply minimizing the cross entropy cost operation that we created. The function will in turn perform gradient descent and backpropagation on your behalf. Before going to the main step, which involves running the operations, let us begin by setting up the variable initialization operation and an operation responsible for measuring the accuracy of the predictions. This can be done as shown below:

 # Setting up the initialisation operator
init_op = tf.global_variables_initializer()
 # Creating the accuracy assessment operation

correct_prediction = tf.equal(tf.argmax(b, 1),
tf.argmax(b_, 1))

accuracy =
tf.reduce_mean(tf.cast(correct_prediction,
tf.float32))

The operation for correct prediction, that is, correct_prediction, makes use of tf.equal function provided by TensorFlow which returns True or False based on whether the arguments supplied to it are equal or not.

The tf.argmax function usually returns the index of maximum element in a tensor/vector. The correct_prediction operation will return a tensor sized (m * 1) of True and False values showing whether the neural network predicted the digit correctly. Our goal is to determine the accuracy of the mean from the tensor. We should begin by casting the type of correct_prediction operation from Boolean to TensorFlow float so as to perform the reduce_mean operation. After doing that, we will have the accuracy operation that can be used for the purpose of assessing the performance of the neural network.

Preparing for Training

We can now prepare for training of the neural network. The full code should be as follows:

```
# Launch the session
with tf.Session() as ses:
  # initializing the variables
  ses.run(init_op)
  total_batch = int(len(mnist.train.labels) /
batch_size)
  for epoch in range(epochs):
    avg_cost = 0
    for x in range(total_batch):

      batch_a, batch_b =
mnist.train.next_batch(batch_size=batch_size)
```

```
    _, z = ses.run([optimiser, cross_entropy],
            feed_dict={a: batch_a, b: batch_b})
    avg_cost += b / total_batch

    print("Epoch:", (epoch + 1), "cost =",
"{:.3f}".format(avg_cost))

    print(ses.run(accuracy, feed_dict={x:
mnist.test.images, b: mnist.test.labels}))
```

The "with" operation has been setup and the initialization operation has been run. The third line is about the mini-batch training scheme that will be run for the neural network. In third line, we have calculated the number of batches that will be run for every epoch.

We have then looped through every epoch then initialized the avg_cost variable to track the average cost entropy cost for every epoch. In the next line, we have extracted the randomized batch of samples, batch_a and batch_b from our training dataset. The MNIST dataset has a utility function named next_batch that facilitates the extraction of batches of data for training.

In the next line, we are running two operations. The ses.run can take a list of operations and run them as its first argument. In such a case, when the [optimiser, cross_entropy] is supplied as the list, the two operations will be performed. This will give us two outputs, which will then be assigned to the variables _ and z.

We are not much concerned about the output we get from the optimizer operation, but we are concerned about the output we get from cross_entropy operation which was assigned to the variable z. The optimizer operation should be run on the batch samples. The z was then used for calculation of the average cost of the epoch.

We have then printed out the progress in average cost, and then once done with training; the accuracy operation was execution to show the accuracy of the trained model on test dataset.

Chapter 3- Working with Images

As you have noticed from our previous examples, TensorFlow comes loaded with some datasets that can be used for deep learning. However, it is still possible for us to load our own data if the one we need to use is not pre-loaded into the TensorFlow. However, the data must be obtained in a format that can be fed into the network.

In this chapter, we will be using a dataset with images of cats and dogs. The work of our neural network will be to differentiate between cats and dogs. The images will be read then kept in a Python list. They will be fed into the network one by one. We only need around 20 images from this dataset.

We will begin by creating a class that will collect images then create a mini batch of about 20 images then use the mini batch to train the neural network. The generator will go ahead to collect another set of images from our folder then create the next mini batch. This should continue until all images in our folder have been used.

Creating the Dataset Generator

The images have stored in a folder named *traindata* and kept in the working directory.
Let us begin by loading the libraries that we will need for our task:

import cv2 # loading the images

import numpy as np # this will help in matrix manipulations

from os.path import isfile, join # to help in manipulating file paths

from os import listdir # to get the files stored in current directory.

from random import shuffle # for shuffling the data (file paths)

We will be using OpenCV for loading the images. One can also use PIL for that purpose, but OpenCV may be a bit easier for this task. For the manipulation of the images, OpenCV will be the best.

Data Separation

The images for the dogs and the cats are kept in the folder. We need to separate them to be in different folders. We simply have to write a function that will help us do that. Here is the function:

```
def seperateData(dir):
  for fname in listdir(dir):
    if isfile(join(dir, fname)):
      tokens = fname.split('.')
      if tokens[-1] == 'jpg':
        image_path = join(dir, fname)
        if not os.path.exists(join(dir, tokens[0])):
```

```
        os.makedirs(join(dir, tokens[0]))

        copyfile(image_path, join(join(dir,
tokens[0]), fname))

        os.remove(image_path)
```

The function will create two folders in the data directory, one named *cat* and the other named *dog*. All the images will then be moved to their corresponding folder.

Note that the above function will only be used for once; hence it should not be included in the data generator class. The reason is that we may never need to use the function again. We can now create the *DataGenerator* class:

```
class DataGenerator:
  def __init__(self, dir):
    self.dir = dir
    self.data_labels = self.get_data_labels()
    self.data_info = self.get_data_paths()
  def get_data_labels(self):
    data_labels = []
    for fname in listdir(self.dir):
      if not isfile(join(self.dir, fname)):
        data_labels.append(fname)
    return data_labels

  def get_data_paths(self):
    data_paths = []
```

```
for label in self.data_labels:
    img_lists=[]
    path = join(self.dir, label)
    for fname in listdir(path):
        tokens = fname.split('.')
        if tokens[-1] == 'jpg':
            image_path=join(path, fname)
            img_lists.append(image_path)
    shuffle(img_lists)
    data_paths.append(img_lists)
return data_paths
```

In the above code, we have created a class named *DataGenerator*. In the initializer part, we have taken the directory with the dataset as the argument and this will help us list all folders contained in the dataset directory. We have also created a list of file paths in the individual directories using the methods *get_data_labels* and *get_data_paths*.

In the method *get_data_lbels*, we have called the *listdir* function which helps us get a list of all items contained in the directory. In our case, the directory should have two items, cat and dog, forming the classes for the dataset.

In the *get_data_path* method, we have also called the *listdir* function. This will return the list of all files and folders contained in the dataset directory. We have used a *for* loop to iterate through them and check whether every path points to a folder or file.

If it points to a file, the path will be split with a dot (.) then check the last token. For a jpeg file, the last token will become a "jpg". This will help in taking the image files and ignore the rest of the files in the directory such as temp files.

After confirming that the file is a JPG file, we have taken the entire path together with the data directory and the class directory as image path.

The image file path has then been appended into the list *img_lists*. The list has then been added to main data_path list. At this point, the data_path list should have two lists, one having the list of image paths for cat and the other with image paths for dog. We now have all image file paths and their corresponding labels. It is now time for us to get the images.

We will use the *generator* concept of Python. The *yield* concept will help us create mini-batches then delete them immediately we have used them to train the network. This way, we will not fill the entire RAM.

Creating Mini-Batch Generator

The mini batch generator for generation of the mini batches can be created as follows:

class DataGenerator:
   ⋮
   ⋮

```python
def get_mini_batches(self, batch_size=10,
image_size=(200, 200), allchannel=True):
    images = []
    labels = []
    empty=False
    counter=0

each_batch_size=int(batch_size/len(self.data_in
fo))
    while True:
      for x in range(len(self.data_labels)):
        label =
np.zeros(len(self.data_labels),dtype=int)
        label[x] = 1
        if len(self.data_info[x]) < counter+1:
          empty=True
          continue
        empty=False
        img =
cv2.imread(self.data_info[x][counter])
        img = self.resizeAndPad(img,
image_size)
        if not allchannel:
        img = cv2.cvtColor(img,
cv2.COLOR_BGR2GRAY)

   img = np.reshape(img, (img.shape[0],
img.shape[1], 1))

        images.append(img)
        labels.append(label)
```

```
        counter+=1

    if empty:
      break

    # In case the iterator is a multiple of the
batch size, return mini batch

    if (counter)%each_batch_size == 0:

      yield np.array(images,dtype=np.uint8),
np.array(labels,dtype=np.uint8)

        del images
        del labels
        images=[]
        labels=[]
```

The generator has been created in the *get_mini_batches* method. We take the *batch_size*, output the *image_size* and the flag *allchannel* checking whether we need to use all 3 channel RGB or simply a gray scale image.

The *batch_size* was first divided into batch_size for every class. This way, we will be able to take equal number of samples from every class. We also have a *counter* to mark the current iteration for every class.

We have then created two lists, that is, images and labels and both are empty. Next, we have started an infinite loop.

The loop will only end once it is realized that there are no images left in any of the classes. Inside our *while* loop, we have initiated the *for* loop that helps us get images from the classes in a one-by-one manner.

This means before we can load any of the images, we should check whether there is any image_path left in our list. This has simply been implemented by checking whether the length of the class is less than the value of the counter.
If this is true, the class is considered to be empty then we proceed to our next class. If this is not the case, the empty flag is set to False then we call the *cv2.imread()* method to load the image.

Our sample images should be of the same size, hence we should change their shape into a square, while taking care not to change their aspect ratio. This will be done using the *resizeAndPad* function from OpenCV.

If the *allchannel* flag is false, we call the *cv2.cvtColor()* to convert the image into gray scale. After that, we obtained a set of images that have been added to the images list and labels list. The counter value was increased by one for the next image.

We have then checked whether the value of empty is true, which means that all the lists have been loaded, after which we will break the *while* loop. If it is not, we proceed to next step.

Every time, the counter is a multiple of *each_batch_size* which is simply the size for the batch of a class. Once done with a yield, the results will be deleted from the memory to release it and continue with adding other data from lists for next call.

Resizing Images

As we had said earlier, we need all images to be of equal size. We will transform them into a square pad but we won't interfere with their aspect ratio. We will use the *resizeAndPad()* method. The code should be as follows:

```
class DataGenerator:
    :
    :
    def resizeAndPad(self, img, size):
        h, w = img.shape[:2]

        sh, sw = size
        # The interpolation method
        if h > sh or w > sw:  # To shrink the image
            interp = cv2.INTER_AREA
        else: # To stretch the image
            interp = cv2.INTER_CUBIC

        # The aspect ratio of the image
        aspect = w/h

        # For padding the image
        if aspect > 1: # The horizontal image
```

```python
        new_shape = list(img.shape)
        new_shape[0] = w
        new_shape[1] = w
        new_shape = tuple(new_shape)
        new_img=np.zeros(new_shape,
dtype=np.uint8)
        h_offset=int((w-h)/2)
        new_img[h_offset:h_offset+h, :, :] =
img.copy()

    elif aspect < 1: # vertical image
        new_shape = list(img.shape)
        new_shape[0] = h
        new_shape[1] = h
        new_shape = tuple(new_shape)
        new_img =
np.zeros(new_shape,dtype=np.uint8)
        w_offset = int((h-w) / 2)
        new_img[:, w_offset:w_offset + w, :] =
img.copy()
    else:
        new_img = img.copy()
    # scale and pad

    scaled_img = cv2.resize(new_img, size,
interpolation=interp)

    return scaled_img
```

We began by checking whether the image should be enlarged or shrink.

The cv2.INTER_AREA method is good for shrinking of images while the *cv2.INTER_CUBIC* is good for enlarging the images.

We have also checked whether the image is vertical or horizontal. We have used zeros to pad it and ensure that it is square. The *cv2.resize* method helps us scale the image to what we need.

The class can now be used for generation of mini batches for the tensorflow model.

The following is the complete code for the model:

```
import cv2
from os.path import isfile, join
import numpy as np
from os import listdir
from shutil import copyfile
import pickle
from random import shuffle
import os


def seperateData(dir):
    for fname in listdir(dir):
        if isfile(join(dir, fname)):
            tokens = fname.split('.')
            if tokens[-1] == 'jpg':
                image_path = join(dir, fname)
                if not os.path.exists(join(dir, tokens[0])):
```

```python
            os.makedirs(join(dir, tokens[0]))
            copyfile(image_path, join(join(dir,
tokens[0]), fname))
            os.remove(image_path)


class DataGenerator:
    def __init__(self, dir):
        self.dir = dir
        self.data_labels = self.get_data_labels()
        self.data_info = self.get_data_paths()

    def get_data_labels(self):
        data_labels = []
        for fname in listdir(self.dir):
            if not isfile(join(self.dir, fname)):
                data_labels.append(fname)
        return data_labels

    def get_data_paths(self):
        data_paths = []
        for label in self.data_labels:
            img_lists=[]
            path = join(self.dir, label)
            for fname in listdir(path):
                tokens = fname.split('.')
                if tokens[-1] == 'jpg':
                    image_path=join(path, fname)
                    img_lists.append(image_path)
            shuffle(img_lists)
            data_paths.append(img_lists)
```

```python
        return data_paths

    def save_labels(self, path):
        pickle.dump(self.data_labels,
open(path,"wb"))

    def get_mini_batches(self, batch_size=10,
image_size=(200, 200), allchannel=True):
        images = []
        labels = []
        empty=False
        counter=0

each_batch_size=int(batch_size/len(self.data_in
fo))
        while True:
            for x in range(len(self.data_labels)):
                label =
np.zeros(len(self.data_labels),dtype=int)
                label[x] = 1
                if len(self.data_info[x]) < counter+1:
                    empty=True
                    continue
                empty=False
                img =
cv2.imread(self.data_info[x][counter])
                img = self.resizeAndPad(img,
image_size)
                if not allchannel:
```

```python
            img = cv2.cvtColor(img,
cv2.COLOR_BGR2GRAY)

            img = np.reshape(img, (img.shape[0],
img.shape[1], 1))

        images.append(img)
        labels.append(label)
    counter+=1

    if empty:
        break

    # if iterator is multiple of a batch size, then
return mini batch

    if (counter)%each_batch_size == 0:
        yield np.array(images,dtype=np.uint8),
np.array(labels,dtype=np.uint8)
        del images
        del labels
        images=[]
        labels=[]

def resizeAndPad(self, img, size):
    h, w = img.shape[:2]

    sh, sw = size
    #An interpolation method
    if h > sh or w > sw:  # To shrink the image
        interp = cv2.INTER_AREA
```

```python
        else: # To stretch the image
            interp = cv2.INTER_CUBIC

        # The image's aspect ratio
        aspect = w/h

        # To pad the image
        if aspect > 1: # The horizontal image
            new_shape = list(img.shape)
            new_shape[0] = w
            new_shape[1] = w
            new_shape = tuple(new_shape)
            new_img=np.zeros(new_shape,
dtype=np.uint8)
            h_offset=int((w-h)/2)
            new_img[h_offset:h_offset+h, :, :] =
img.copy()
        elif aspect < 1: # The vertical image
            new_shape = list(img.shape)
            new_shape[0] = h
            new_shape[1] = h
            new_shape = tuple(new_shape)
            new_img =
np.zeros(new_shape,dtype=np.uint8)
            w_offset = int((h-w) / 2)
            new_img[:, w_offset:w_offset + w, :] =
img.copy()
        else:
            new_img = img.copy()
        #To scale and pad
```

```python
    scaled_img = cv2.resize(new_img, size,
interpolation=interp)
    return scaled_img

if __name__=="__main__":
  seperateData("./traindata")
```

For the code to run, ensure that you have all the necessary libraries, that is, the ones at the beginning of the code added via *import* statement.

Chapter 4- Importing Data

There are various ways through which data can be passed to TensorFlow. One of these ways is *feed-dict* but it should be avoided as it is slow. An input pipeline is the best way of passing data to TensorFlow as it ensures that there is no waiting for new stuff to come in.

TensorFlow comes with an API known as *Dataset* that can help perform this task with ease. In this chapter, we will be showing you how to create an input pipeline and feed data into your model more efficiently.

There are three steps needed for one to use a dataset. They include the following:

1. Import the data
This involves the creation of an instance of a Dataset from the data.

2. Create an Iterator
This involves the use of the created dataset to create an iterator instance for iterating through the dataset.

3. Consuming Data
We can use the iterator that has been created to get elements from our dataset and feed them into the model.

Importing Data from numpy

It occurs that one has a numpy array which they need to pass to TensorFlow. This can be done as shown below:

```
# create a random vector with shape (100,2)
i = np.random.sample((100,2))
#create a dataset from numpy array
dataset = tf.data.Dataset.from_tensor_slices(i)
```

It is also possible for us to pass more than one numpy arrays to the TensorFlow. A good example of this is when we have data that has been divided into characteristics and labels. This is demonstrated below:

```
characteristics, labels =
(np.random.sample((100,2)),
np.random.sample((100,1)))
dataset =
tf.data.Dataset.from_tensor_slices((characteristi
cs, labels))
```

Initializing Data in Tensors

It is possible for us to initialize the dataset with a tensor. Here is an example:

```
# using some tensor
dataset =
tf.data.Dataset.from_tensor_slices(tf.random_u
niform([100, 2]))
```

Getting Data from Placeholder

This becomes applicable when we are in need of dynamically changing the data contained in the dataset. This is demonstrated below:

```
i = tf.placeholder(tf.float32, shape=[None,2])
dataset = tf.data.Dataset.from_tensor_slices(i)
```

Getting Data from Generator

It is possible for us to initialize a dataset from a generator. This becomes applicable when we have an array whose elements have a different length. It can be done as demonstrated below:

```
import numpy as np
import tensorflow as tf
# using the generator
sequence =
np.array([[[23]],[[2],[569]],[[73],[42],[9312]]])
def generator():
  for x in sequence:
    yield x

dataset =
tf.data.Dataset().batch(1).from_generator(gener
ator,

      output_types= tf.int64,
```

```
  output_shapes=(tf.TensorShape([None, 1])))
iter = dataset.make_initializable_iterator()
x = iter.get_next()
with tf.Session() as ses:
  ses.run(iter.initializer)
  print(ses.run(x))
  print(ses.run(x))
  print(ses.run(x))
```

The above will generate the following data for us:

```
      [[23]]
      [[   2]
       [569]]
      [[   73]
       [   42]
       [9312]]
```

You are required to define the types and the shapes of your data for use in creation of correct tensors.

Importing Data from CSV

You are allowed to read a csv (comma separated values) into your dataset. To create a dataset from a csv file, you should call the *tf.contrib.data.make_csv_dataset* method. The iterator will then create a dictionary with a key as column names and values as Tensor with correct row value. In my case, I have the file named *myfile.csv*. I can create a dataset from it as follows:

import tensorflow as tf

```
# loading a csv file
CSV_PATH = './myfile.csv'
dataset =
tf.contrib.data.make_csv_dataset(CSV_PATH,
batch_size=32)
iterat = dataset.make_one_shot_iterator()
next = iterat.get_next()
print(next)

# next is the dict with key=columns names and
value=column data
inputs, labels = next['text'], next['sentiment']

with  tf.Session() as ses:
    ses.run([inputs, labels])
```

Creating an Iterator

After loading the dataset, we need to use an iterator that will iterate through the dataset to get the real values. There are four different types of iterators that one can create:

1. One shot
This can iterate through a dataset for only once, and you are not allowed to feed ay value to it.

2. Initializable
You are allowed to dynamically change the calling of its initializer operation and passing new data via *feed_dict*. It can be viewed as a bucket that one can fill with items.

3. Reinitializable
This one may be initialized from a different dataset. It is well applicable in cases where one has a training dataset that needs to be transformed further.

4. Feedable

This may help in choosing the iterator that is to be used.

One Shot Iterator

This is the simplest iterator one can create. It can be created as demonstrated below:

import tensorflow as tf
import numpy as np

i = np.random.sample((100,2))
 # create a dataset from numpy array
dataset = tf.data.Dataset.from_tensor_slices(i)

 # creating the iterator
iterat = dataset.make_one_shot_iterator()

Next, you should call the *get_next()* method that will in turn call the tensor with the data. This is shown below:

...
 # creating the iterator
iterat = dataset.make_one_shot_iterator()
a = iter.get_next()

We can now call the a then see the value stored in it:

with tf.Session() as ses:
**   print(ses.run(a))**
Initializable Iterator

We can come up with a dataset with a placeholder in cases when we need create a dynamic dataset on which the data source can be changed at runtime. The placeholder may be initialized via the *feed-dict* method. Here is an example:

```
# using the placeholder
i = tf.placeholder(tf.float32, shape=[None,2])
dataset = tf.data.Dataset.from_tensor_slices(i)
data = np.random.sample((100,2))
iterat = dataset.make_initializable_iterator()
# creating the iterator
 = iterat.get_next()

with tf.Session() as ses:
    # feed data to the placeholder
    ses.run(iterat.initializer, feed_dict={ i: data })
    print(ses.run(a))
```

We have called the *make_initializable_iterator*. Inside the scope of *ses,* we ran the *initializer* operation so as to pass the data, which is a random numpy array. We have both the train and test datasets:

```
traindata = (np.random.sample((100,2)),
np.random.sample((100,1)))
testdata = (np.array([[1,2]]), np.array([[0]]))
```

We train the model then test it using the test data. We do this by initializing the iterator again once done with the training. This is shown below:

```
# Initializable iterator for switching between
dataset
EPOCHS = 10

a, b = tf.placeholder(tf.float32, shape=[None,2]),
tf.placeholder(tf.float32, shape=[None,1])
dataset = tf.data.Dataset.from_tensor_slices((a,
b))

traindata = (np.random.sample((100,2)),
np.random.sample((100,1)))
testdata = (np.array([[1,2]]), np.array([[0]]))

iterat = dataset.make_initializable_iterator()
characteristics, labels = iterat.get_next()

with tf.Session() as ses:
#    Initializing the iterator with the train data
   ses.run(iterat.initializer, feed_dict={ a:
traindata[0], b: traindata[1]})
   for _ in range(EPOCHS):
     ses.run([characteristics, labels])
#    switching to the test data
```

```
    ses.run(iterat.initializer, feed_dict={ a:
testdata[0], b: testdata[1]})
    print(ses.run([characteristics, labels]))
```

Reinitializable Iterator

Our goal is to be able to switch between data dynamically. Instead of having to feed a new data to a similar dataset, we only switch the dataset. We need both the train and the test dataset as follows:

```
# create fake data with numpy
traindata = (np.random.sample((100,2)),
np.random.sample((100,1)))
testdata = (np.random.sample((10,2)),
np.random.sample((10,1)))
```

Let us create two datasets:

```
# creating two datasets, one traindata and one for
testdata
traindataset =
tf.data.Dataset.from_tensor_slices(traindata)
testdataset =
tf.data.Dataset.from_tensor_slices(testdata)
```

The trick is in the creation of a generic iterator:

```
# creating an iterator for correct shape and type
iterat =
tf.data.Iterator.from_structure(traindataset.out
put_types, traindataset.output_shapes)
```

The above should be followed by the creation of two initialization operations:

creating the initialization operations
train_init_op =
iterat.make_initializer(traindataset)
test_init_op =
iterat.make_initializer(testdataset)

Let us grab the next element:

characteristics, labels = iterat.get_next()

We can now use our session to run the two initialization operations directly:

After putting the code together, we end up with the following:

A reinitializable iterator for switching between
Datasets
EPOCHS = 10
# creating fake data with numpy
traindata = (np.random.sample((100,2)),
np.random.sample((100,1)))
testdata = (np.random.sample((10,2)),
np.random.sample((10,1)))
# creating two datasets for training and for
testing
traindataset =

```
tf.data.Dataset.from_tensor_slices(traindata)
testdataset =
tf.data.Dataset.from_tensor_slices(testdata)
# creating an iterator of correct shape and type
iterat =
tf.data.Iterator.from_structure(traindataset.out
put_types,

traindataset.output_shapes)
characteristics, labels = iterat.get_next()
# creating initialization operations
train_init_op =
iterat.make_initializer(traindataset)
test_init_op =
iterat.make_initializer(testdataset)
with tf.Session() as ses:
   ses.run(train_init_op) # switching to the train
dataset
   for _ in range(EPOCHS):
     ses.run([characteristics, labels])
   ses.run(test_init_op) # switching to the val
dataset
   print(ses.run([characteristics, labels]))
```

Feedable Iterator

This is almost the same as the reinitializable iterator, but instead of switching between datasets, it switches between iterators. Let us begin by creating two datasets, one for training and another one for testing:

traindataset = tf.data.Dataset.from_tensor_slices((a,b))
testdataset = tf.data.Dataset.from_tensor_slices((a,b))

We can now create the iterator using the *initializable* iterator. However, it is still possible for you to use the one shot iterator:

trainiterator = traindataset.make_initializable_iterator()
testiterator = testdataset.make_initializable_iterator()

We should now create a handle that will be used as a placeholder for use as a placeholder capable of being changed dynamically. The handle can be created as follows:

handle = tf.placeholder(tf.string, shape=[])

We can then create a generic iterator by use of the dataset shape. This is shown below:

iterat = tf.data.Iterator.from_string_handle(

  handle, traindataset.output_types, traindataset.output_shapes)

We can now get our next elements:

next_elements = iterat.get_next()

For us to switch between operators, we should call the operation named *next_elements* and pass the correct handle to *feed-dict*. Here is an example showing how we can get an element from train set:

ses.run(next_elements, feed_dict = {handle: train_handle})

For the users of initializable operators, don't forget to initialize them before you start. This can be done as follows:

ses.run(train_iterator.initializer, feed_dict={ a: traindata[0], b: traindata[1]})

ses.run(test_iterator.initializer, feed_dict={ a: testdata[0], b: testdata[1]})

After putting all of them together, we will end up with the following:

 # A feedable iterator for switching between iterators
EPOCHS = 10
 # creating fake data with numpy
traindata = (np.random.sample((100,2)),
np.random.sample((100,1)))
testdata = (np.random.sample((10,2)),
np.random.sample((10,1)))

```python
# creating a placeholder
a, b = tf.placeholder(tf.float32, shape=[None,2]),
tf.placeholder(tf.float32, shape=[None,1])

# creating two datasets, for training and for
testing
traindataset =
tf.data.Dataset.from_tensor_slices((a,b))
testdataset =
tf.data.Dataset.from_tensor_slices((a,b))
# creating iterators from dataset
train_iterator =
traindataset.make_initializable_iterator()
test_iterator =
testdataset.make_initializable_iterator()

handle = tf.placeholder(tf.string, shape=[])
iterat = tf.data.Iterator.from_string_handle(
    handle, traindataset.output_types,
traindataset.output_shapes)
next_elements = iterat.get_next()
with tf.Session() as ses:
    train_handle =
ses.run(train_iterator.string_handle())
    test_handle =
ses.run(test_iterator.string_handle())

    # initializing the iterators.
    ses.run(train_iterator.initializer, feed_dict={
a: traindata[0], b: traindata[1]})
    ses.run(test_iterator.initializer, feed_dict={ a:
```

```
testdata[0], b: testdata[1]})

    for _ in range(EPOCHS):
      a, b = ses.run(next_elements, feed_dict =
{handle: train_handle})
       print(a, b)

    a,b = ses.run(next_elements, feed_dict =
{handle: test_handle})
    print(a,b)
```

Using the Data

We have been using the session to get the value of *next* element in our dataset:

```
...
next_el = iterat.get_next()
...
print(ses.run(next_el)) # will return the current element
```

For us to pass data to the model, we should pass the tensors that were generated from *get_next()*. In the following code, we have a dataset with two numpy arrays:

```
# use of two numpy arrays
characteristics, labels =
(np.array([np.random.sample((100,2))]),

np.array([np.random.sample((100,1))]))
```

dataset = tf.data.Dataset.from_tensor_slices((characteristics,labels)).repeat().batch(BATCH_SIZE)

Next, we create the iterator:

iterat = dataset.make_one_shot_iterator()
a, b = iterat.get_next()

Let us then create a simple neural network model:

 # creating a simple model

net = tf.layers.dense(a, 8) # pass the first value from iter.get_next() as input

net = tf.layers.dense(net, 8)
prediction = tf.layers.dense(net, 1)
loss = tf.losses.mean_squared_error(prediction, b)
 # pass the second value from iterat.get_net() as label
train_op = tf.train.AdamOptimizer().minimize(loss)

We can then directly use the tensors we get from *iter.get_next()* as input to first layer and as labels for loss function. Let's put all together:

import tensorflow as tf

```
import numpy as npEPOCHS = 10
BATCH_SIZE = 16
# use of two numpy arrays
characteristics, labels =
(np.array([np.random.sample((100,2))]),

np.array([np.random.sample((100,1))]))

dataset =
tf.data.Dataset.from_tensor_slices((characteristi
cs,labels)).repeat().batch(BATCH_SIZE)

iterat = dataset.make_one_shot_iterator()
a, b = iterat.get_next()
# creating a simple model
net = tf.layers.dense(a, 8, activation=tf.tanh) #
pass first value from iterat.get_next() as input
net = tf.layers.dense(net, 8, activation=tf.tanh)
prediction = tf.layers.dense(net, 1,
activation=tf.tanh)
loss = tf.losses.mean_squared_error(prediction,
b) # passing second value from iterat.get_net() as
label
train_op =
tf.train.AdamOptimizer().minimize(loss)
with tf.Session() as ses:
    ses.run(tf.global_variables_initializer())
    for x in range(EPOCHS):
        _, loss_value = ses.run([train_op, loss])
        print("Iterat: {}, Loss: {:.4f}".format(x,
loss_value))
```

The code will return the following:

```
Iterat: 0, Loss: 0.2130
Iterat: 1, Loss: 0.2042
Iterat: 2, Loss: 0.1958
Iterat: 3, Loss: 0.1878
Iterat: 4, Loss: 0.1803
Iterat: 5, Loss: 0.1732
Iterat: 6, Loss: 0.1665
Iterat: 7, Loss: 0.1603
Iterat: 8, Loss: 0.1545
Iterat: 9, Loss: 0.1491
. . .
```

Conclusion

This marks the end of this book. TensorFlow is a library for deep learning. It can be used in various computer programming languages including Python. In Python, this library can be installed using pip from the command line. Note that pip is installed together with Python. The library comes with a number of datasets that you can use for deep learning. You can use the inbuilt datasets or load your own dataset into TensorFlow.

TensorFlow allows you to create neural network computer models. These are computer models whose operation is inspired by the way the human brain works. Once created, one trains them with data before using them to make predictions.

www.ingramcontent.com/pod-product-compliance
Lightning Source LLC
Chambersburg PA
CBHW070858070326
40690CB00009B/1904